Dick Taylor
Andy Brend

Real Weathering
A Reference for Military Modellers
Vol. 2

STRATUS

Published in Poland in 2025
by STRATUS s.j.
ul. Żeromskiego 6A,
27-600 Sandomierz, Poland
e-mail: office@mmpbooks.biz
as
MMPBooks,
© 2025 MMPBooks.
http://www.mmpbooks.biz

All rights reserved. Apart from any fair dealing for the purpose of private study, research, criticism or review, as permitted under the Copyright, Design and Patents Act, 1988, no part of this publication may be reproduced, stored in a retrieval system, or transmitted in any form or by any means, electronic, electrical, chemical, mechanical, optical, photocopying, recording or otherwise, without prior written permission. All enquiries should be addressed to the publisher.

ISBN
978-83-67227-83-4

Editor in chief
Roger Wallsgrove

Editorial Team
Robert Pęczkowski
Artur Juszczak

DTP
Stratus sp. j.

Printed by
**Drukarnia
Sowa Sp. z o.o.**
ul. Raszyńska 13
05-500 Piaseczno

PRINTED IN POLAND

Table of contents

Acknowledgements 2
Introduction 3
     Reviews for Volume 1 5
Dirt and Dust 9
Wheels & Wheeled Chassis 40
Engines, Electrical Equipment & Instruments 68
Engineer and Plant Vehicles 92
Glass and Sights 108
Extreme Rust 118
Miscellaneous 133

Acknowledgements

    The majority of images are from Dick Taylor and Andy Brend, with additional material from Richard Stickland and MMP. All web-sourced images are noted as open source.

Introduction

This is the second book in a series about weathering and designed with one main audience in mind – the military modeller. As we all know, there are many books concerned with weathering military models available, but they all concentrate on weathering techniques – pre-shading, washes, pin-washes, dry-brushing, hairspray, you name it, it has a name and a technique. This series is different: it does not tell the modeller how to achieve a particular finish. Rather, it is a reference series showing a range of real military vehicles and their components in real military environments. This series is therefore primarily a reference source for modellers who wish to study real vehicles in real service conditions and faithfully reproduce what happens in real life. Naturally, virtually all of the images shown here are of modern vehicles. Almost no colour photographs exist of the First World War – those that do are generally artificially colorized – and even during the Second World War black and white images far outnumber colour versions. WW2 (and earlier) vehicles do still exist in fair numbers, but they are generally either in museums or in the hands of private experts and collectors who prefer their vehicles to be stowed realistically but not to be covered in mud and dirt and dust and rust – the very things that make them representative of real service are the same things that destroy surfaces and eat away at metal, wood and canvas. Weathering, if we may use the term, is a bad thing for those seeking to preserve. That does not mean that military vehicle shows are not useful for the modeller, far from it. But it would be unwise to expect to see these prized and valuable historical artefacts – for that is what they all are – replicating real service conditions, even after a typical arena display.

Deserts are a favourite area for modellers to start to depict terrain, as they are relatively simple. It is worth remembering that military training areas often take on the appearance of sandy deserts after years of trials and exercises. This is Bovington in Dorset in the south of England, an extremely popular tourist area that would not be so attractive if it all looked like this!

And even reference books like this can only go so far. One criticism that we are bound to hear is that there are no images of an M551 Sheridan, of a Panzer III Ausf L, or an AMX 30. That of course is to miss the point. There is nothing like real experience to inform the modellers' choice of finish, which can then be based upon personal knowledge rather than research. But how to gain that knowledge and experience if one has never served in the military? Well, in part the answer is simple – it is not just military vehicles that gather dust and mud, or rust if not looked after properly, or that suffer damage and neglect. In particular, there are two classes of civilian vehicles that exhibit similar weathering. These are those used on farms and in agriculture, and construction and plant vehicles. So, the message is this: take every opportunity to look at these vehicles in real life, preferably with a camera to hand, and build up your own reference library. And beyond these two obvious sources of inspiration, remember that all vehicles get grubby to some degree, and these can be equally valuable sources of inspiration. Some of the photos in this series were taken by me when walking around my local area, so you do not need to travel far to be inspired.

Another tip is to categorise the effects that you see or are interested in, which can vary from very light (hardly dirty at all) to extremely heavy, usually meaning scrapped vehicles that have been left exposed to the elements for decades. Such categories could be done by effect: for example, rust; dirt; mud; mud and grass; soot; dust; fuel, oil and grease; rain streaks; paint chipping; brick dust; and even moss and lichen growth. Or they could be done by vehicle type: tracked; tank; APC; wheeled; motorcycles; etc, or by vehicle component: suspension; engine and transmission; weapons; markings etc. The point that I am making is that you know what types of vehicles and periods you are most interested in and can tailor your references to suit.

It is to be hoped that the two volumes in this series will aid modellers in achieving the finish that they desire. Hopefully, these books will go a long way to providing a ready reference for weathering effects, and we are always open to suggestions for those categories that we have so far omitted. I am actively considering what else might be useful references for modellers, and I am drawn to the idea of further volumes covering details for diorama creators – brickwork, buildings, roads and tracks, fences, infrastructure and the like – please contact the publisher if you think that these would be useful.

Water and Mud. A Challenger 2 tackles a water obstacle on an exercise – note how the tracks throw up chunks of dirt and mud high into the area, and also how the green camouflage paint is almost obscured by the layers of dust.

Reviews for Volume 1

ARMORAMA: "This is a must have book for anyone who wants to learn where to apply weathering and how much weathering to apply. The pictures show exactly where goop accumulates around the tracks, wheels and other recessed areas, where rust accumulates and what a faded canvas looks like. The author states there will be a volume two in the Realistic Weathering series covering more dirt and grime as well as engineering vehicles, glass, tools and wheeled vehicle suspensions. This book is Highly Recommended for anyone looking for help with weathering realistically."

AMPS-ARMOR.ORG: "When I first open this title I was not expecting much, but I have to compliment the quality of the images and the idea behind the title. Nothing explains the state that vehicles get into than photographs of actual vehicles as it takes away the 'It's not natural or realistic' retorts. I have to say that some of the patterns or patinas that appear I never would have believed and so this title is one worth adding to the library when it comes to painting and finishing."

Modern military wheeled vehicles are almost as equally at home tackling cross-country terrain as their tracked counterparts. This Fuchs is simultaneously muddy, dusty, and wet. Note how the design of the hull helps to keep the worst of the mud below the "waistline".

Effects can be limited to certain areas only; this 432 has got a very dusty suspension and sides, but the remainder of the hull is remarkably clean.

Another really dirty vehicle. It is not unknown for the crew of such a vehicle to slowly and deliberately tackle a water obstacle – or even to sit in it for a few minutes - to try to clean the worst of the grime from the suspension if a washdown is not available. Despite appearances, most crews will try to keep their vehicles as clean as possible.

Engineer vehicles tend to get grubbier than most others, due to their role. This will include stowage items, such as the camouflage net, other parts of the vehicle, like the fascine pipes at the rear – and of course the crew!

The callsign 17D will be almost impossible to read at a range of over fifty meters or so, which makes it useless in a tactical setting. And did anyone spot the soldier on the bank? His MTP camouflage is extremely effective, only his hands draw attention to his presence.

This Warrior does not like it has been out on exercise for very long, as it is remarkably clean. However, if we were to look at the same vehicle a few days later, it would almost certainly look very different!

Protected Military Vehicles are not meant to spend long periods moving across complex terrain, and try to stick to tracks and thus tend to stay a bit cleaner than their tactical counterparts like tanks and APCs. Although this vehicle looks extremely clean, close inspection will reveal a light coating of grey dust over the Light Stone paintwork.

A variety of effects on display as this tank reverses at speed on Salisbury Plain training area.

Operating in such conditions is painful for the tank crews, as the mud will make suspension maintenance dirty and difficult, and it will be almost impossible to stop the mud being tramped inside the cab and fighting compartment. It is probable that these Queen's Dragoon Guards crews in Bosnia in 1996 have parked close alongside each other so that they can jump from tank to tank!

AS90 SPGs prepare to fire. The camouflage netting is pretty effective at breaking up the shape of the turret, although the barrels are a bit of a give-away. Note the leaking oil hub on one of the roadwheels.

Crews sometimes get weathered too! Note also how the driver's periscope is now rendered useless by the mud on it, so the crew need to carry out some local cleaning as soon as possible.

Dirt and Dust

11

15

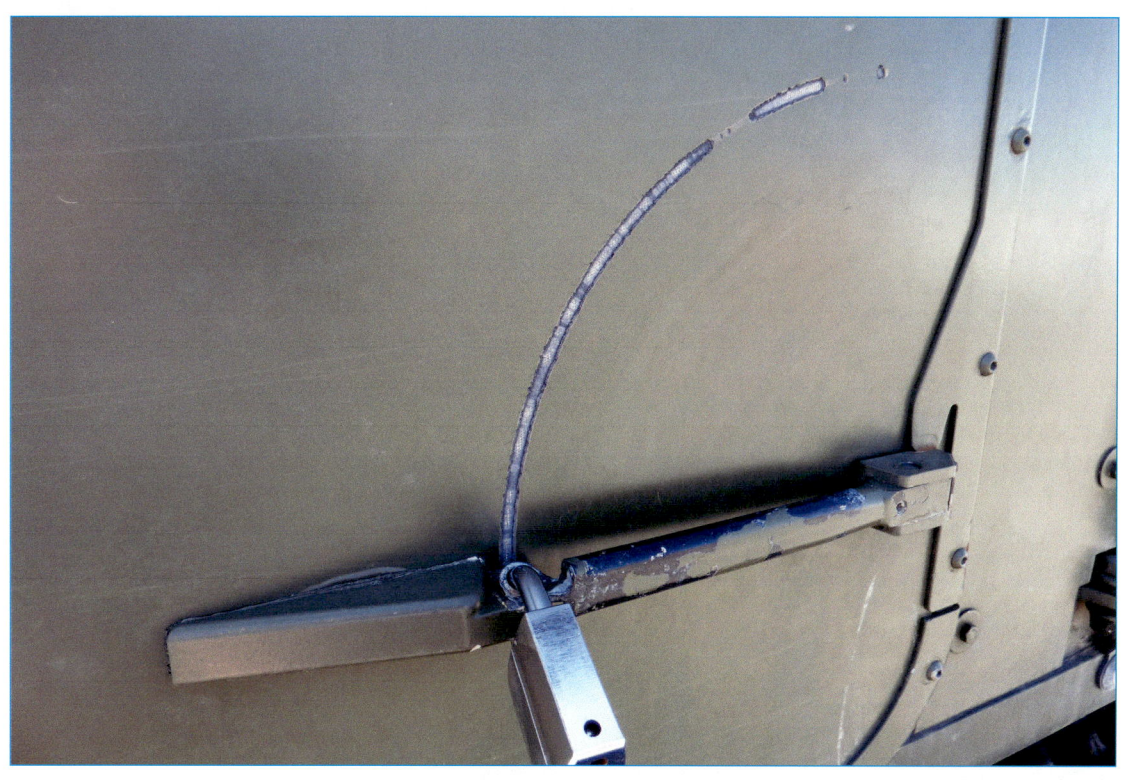

24

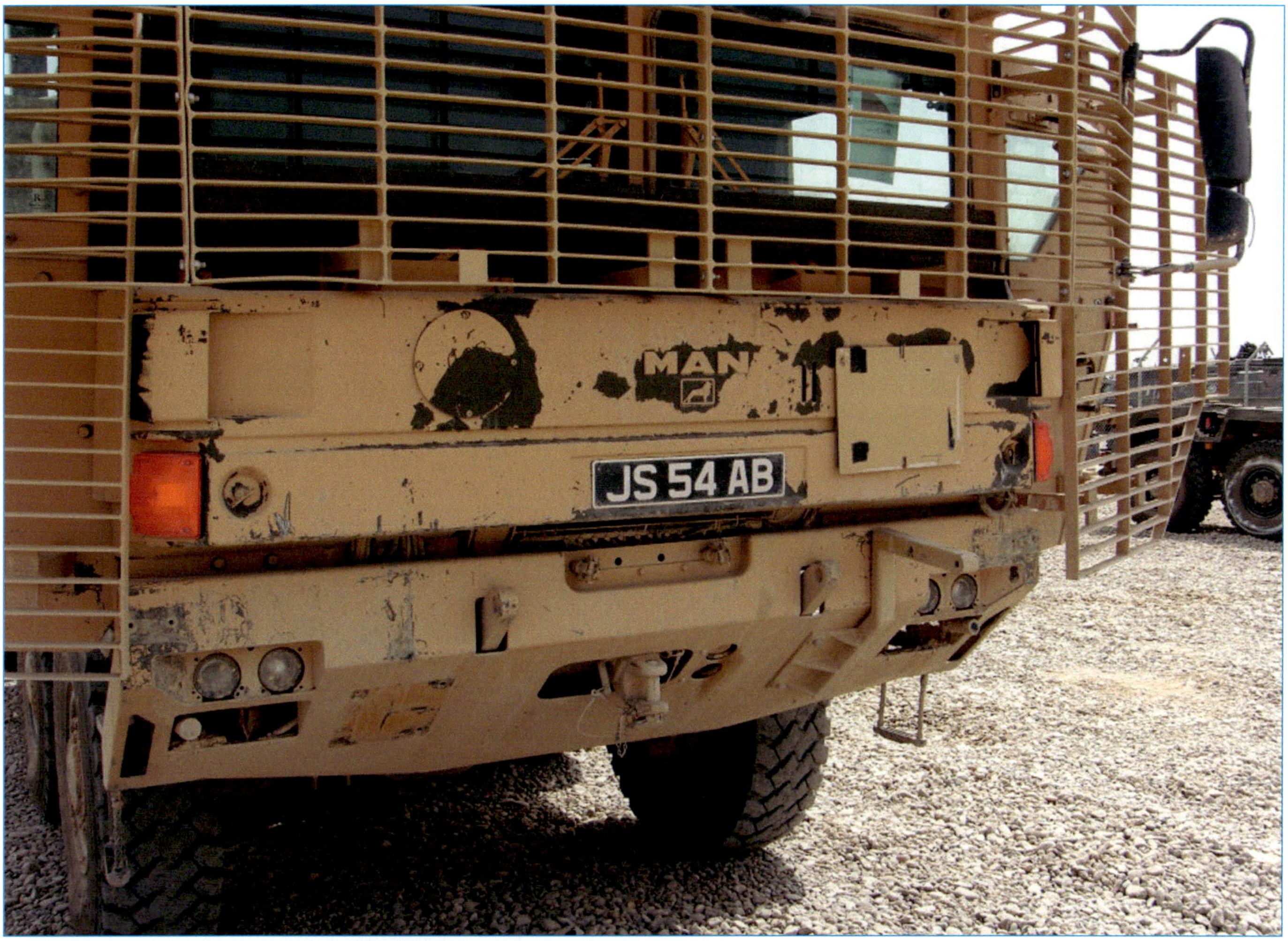
MAN
JS 54 AB

VEHICLE NTWY
EX 23 AB

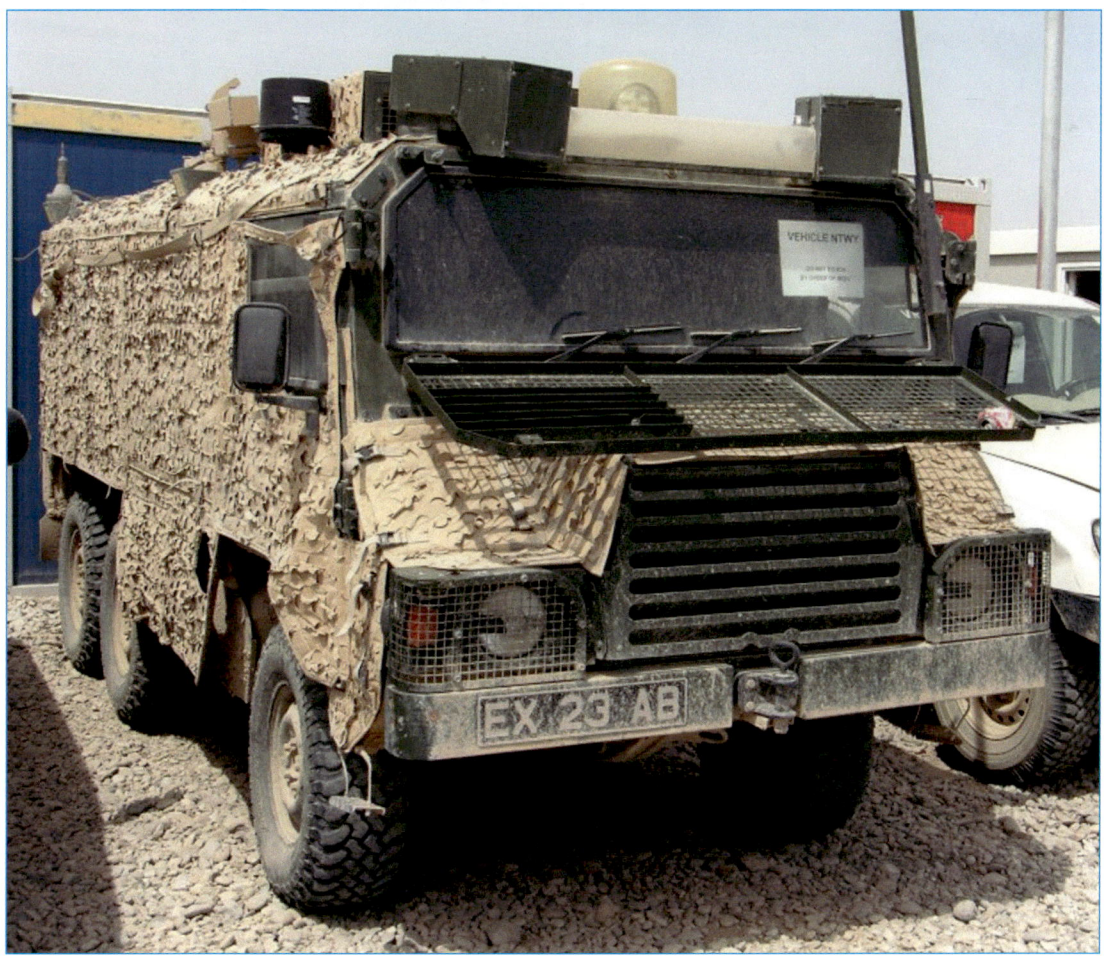

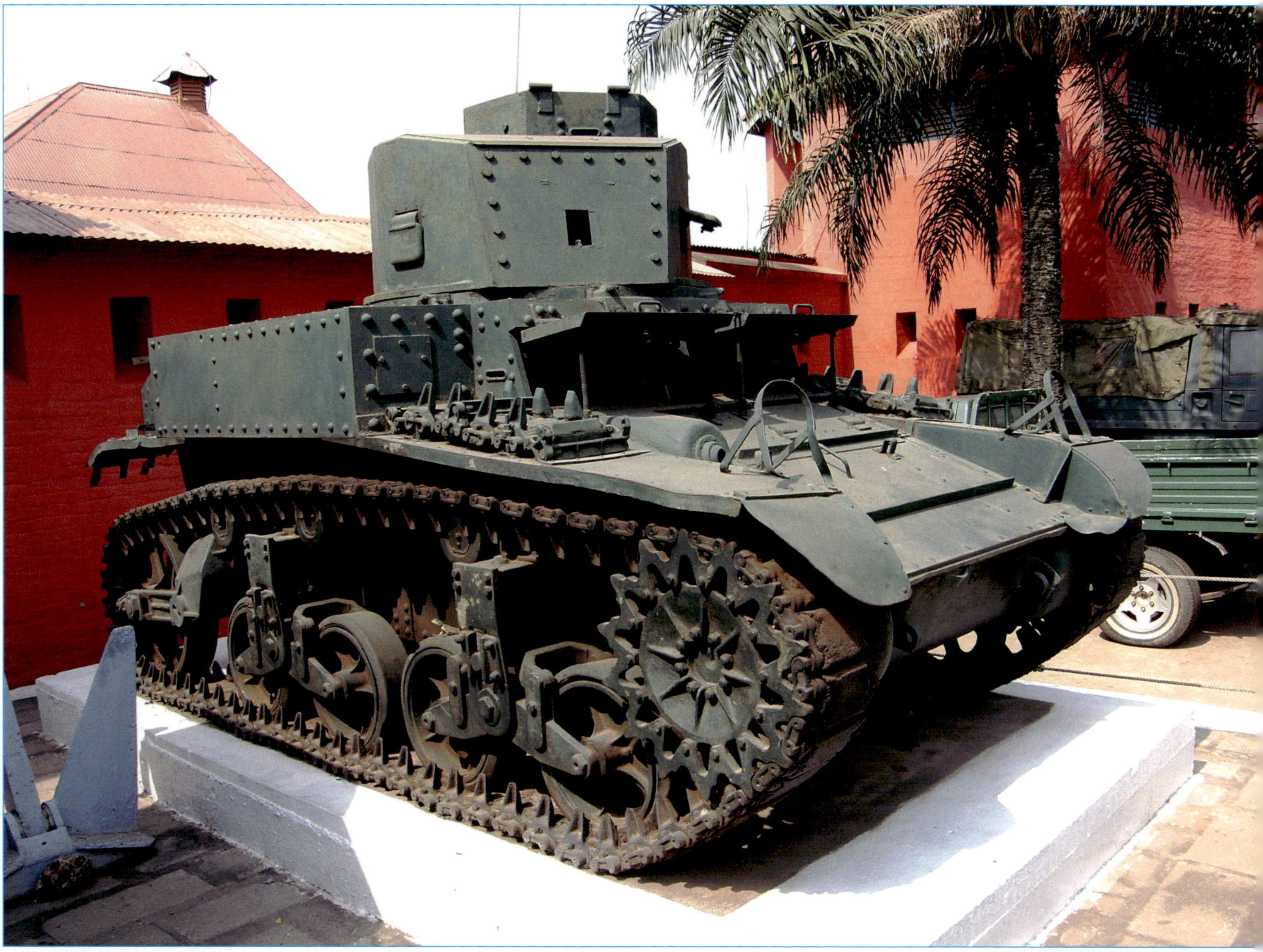

ARMED FORCES MUSEUM
MUSEE DES
FORCES ARMEES

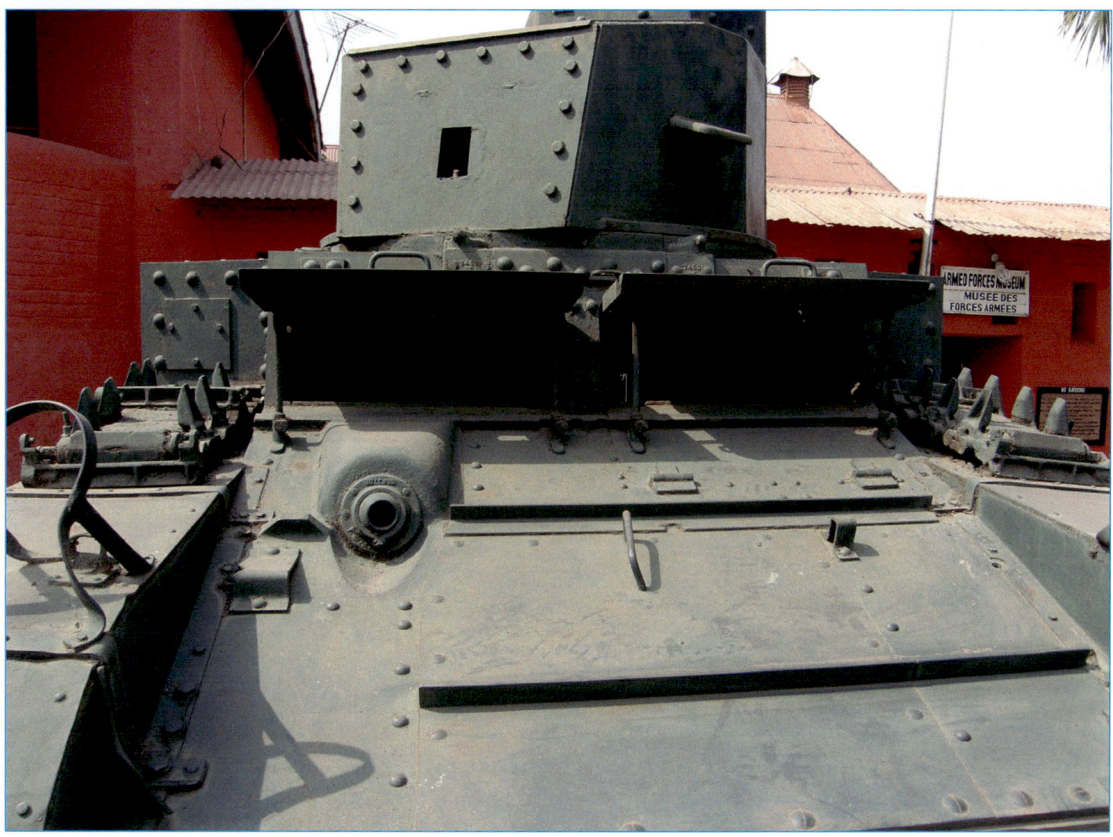

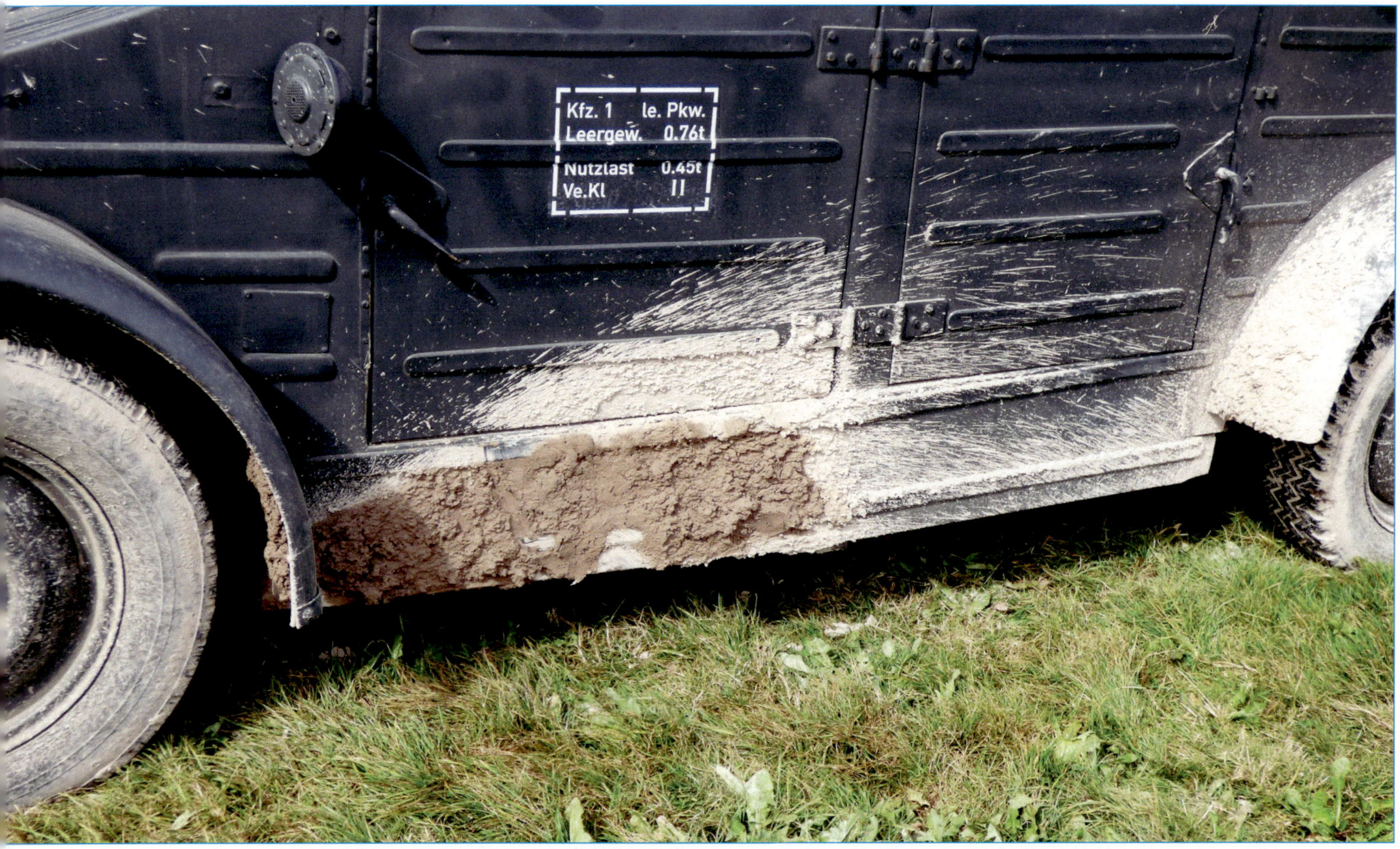
Kfz. 1 le. Pkw.
Leergew. 0.76t
Nutzlast 0.45t
Ve.Kl II

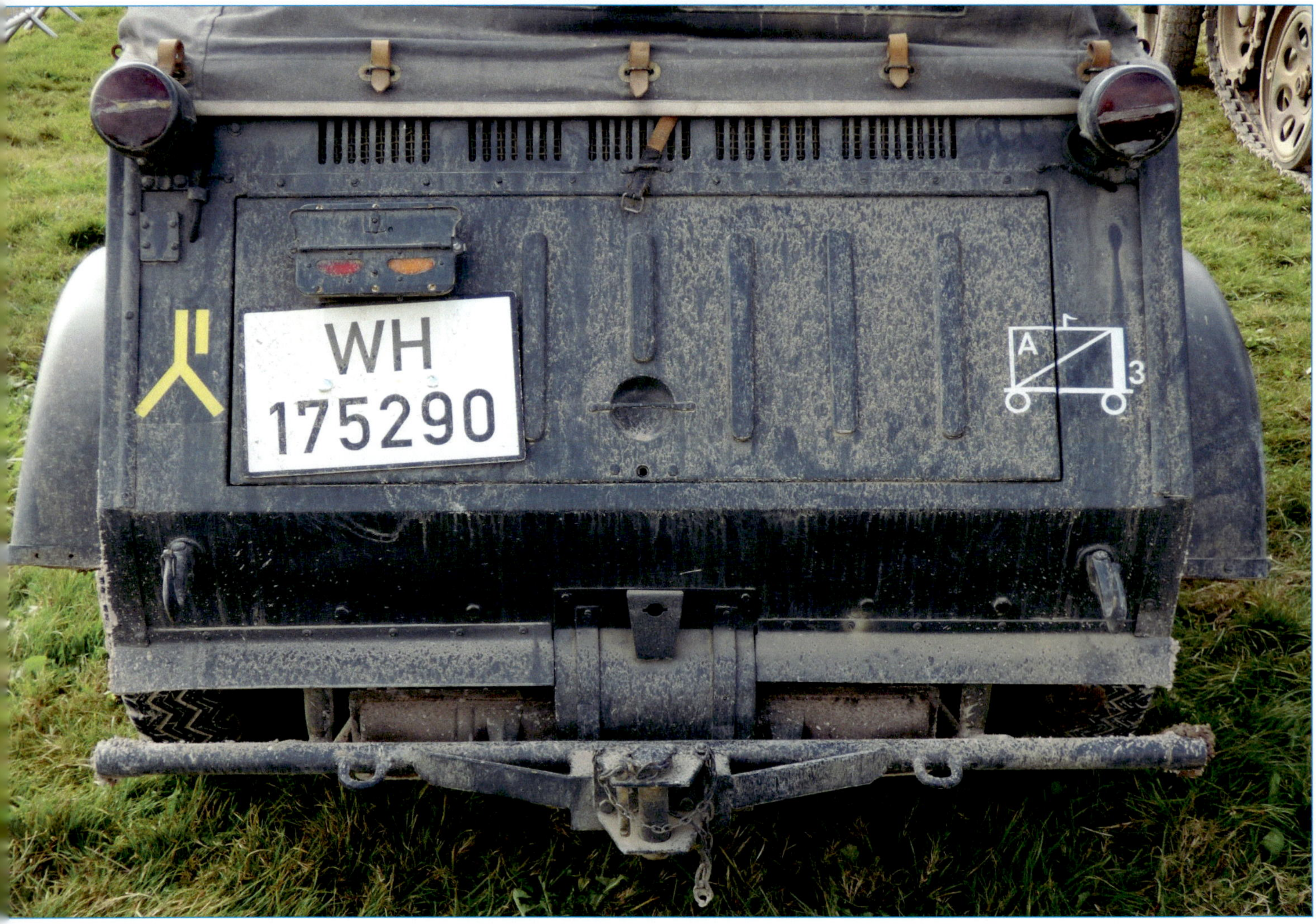
WH
175290
A
3

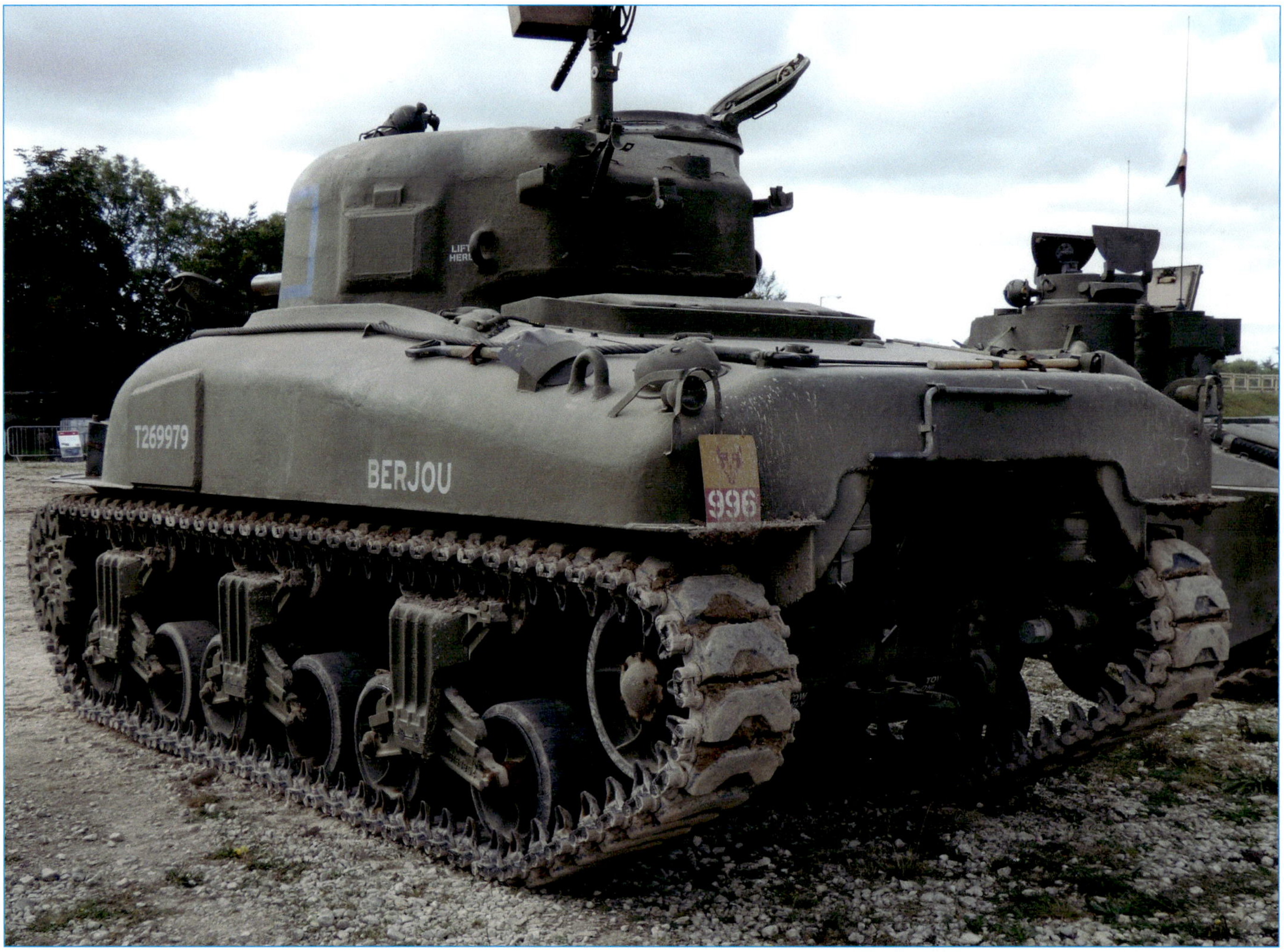

Wheels & Wheeled Chassis

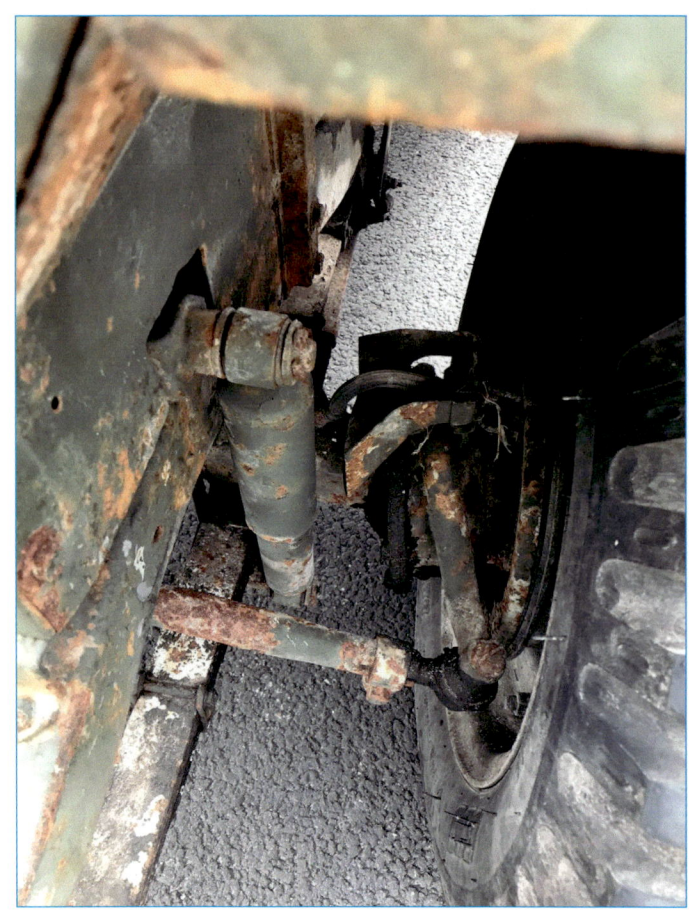

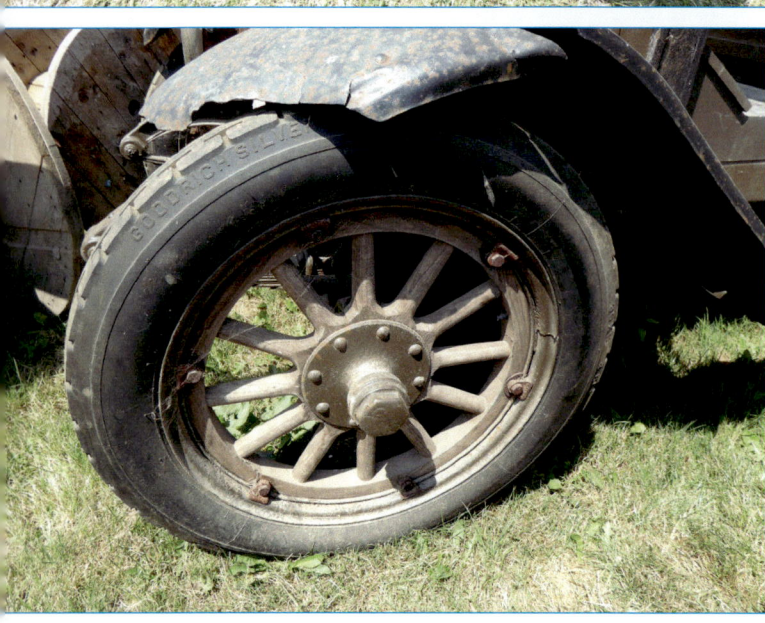

56

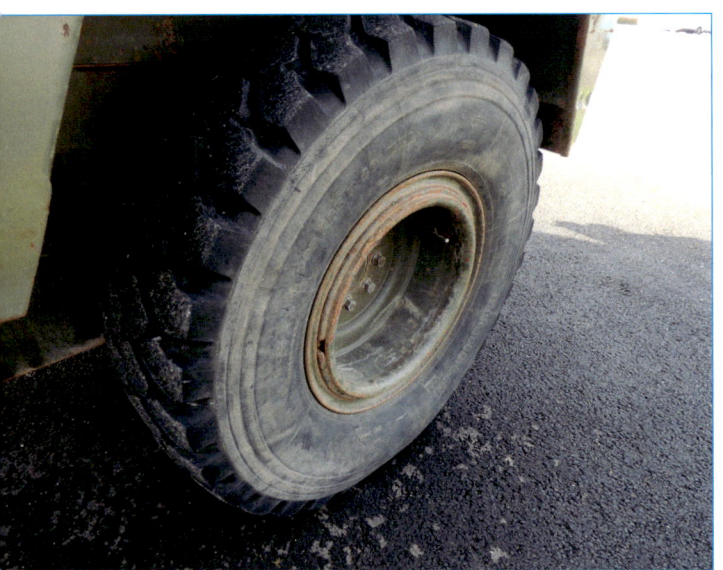

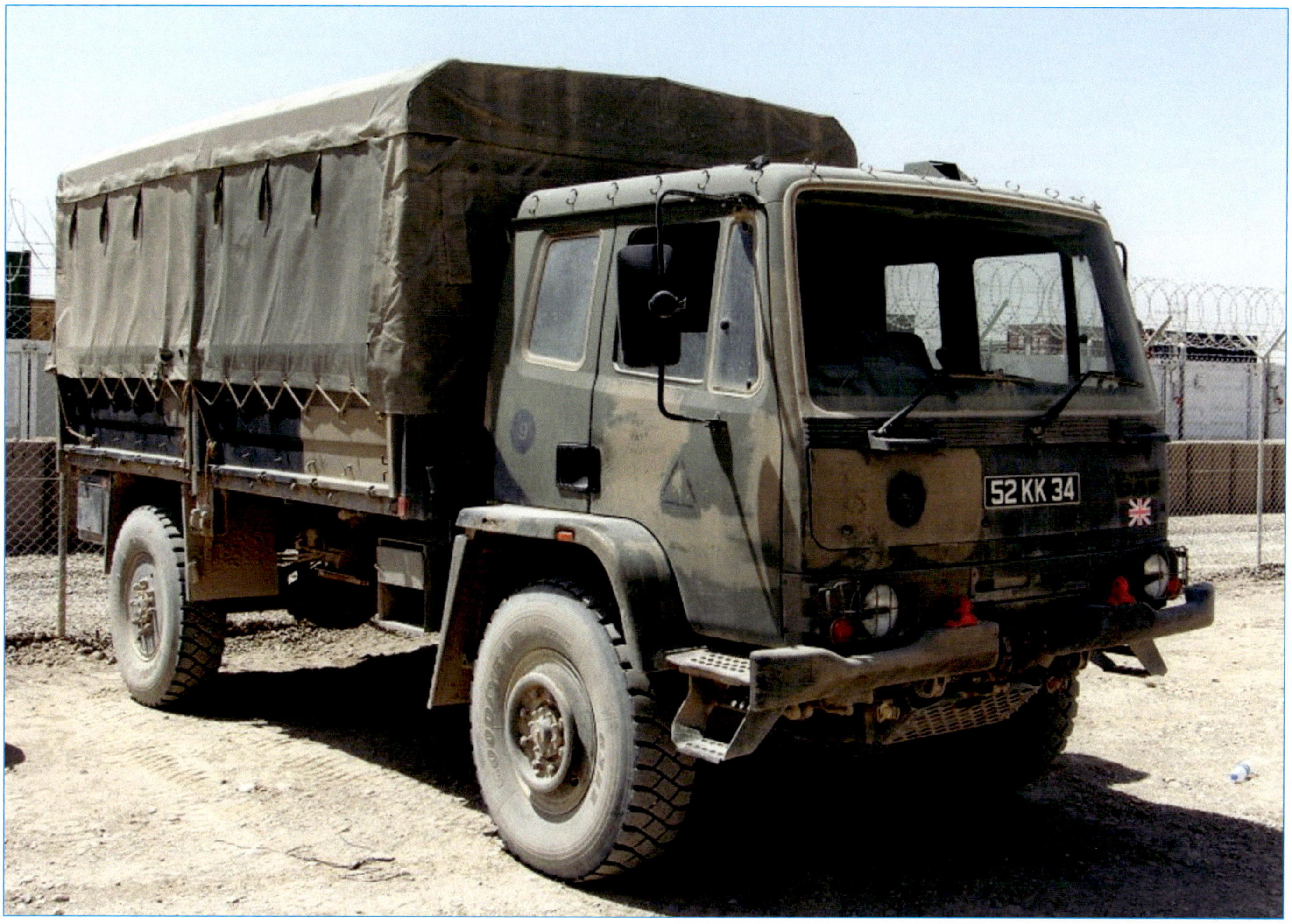
52 KK 34

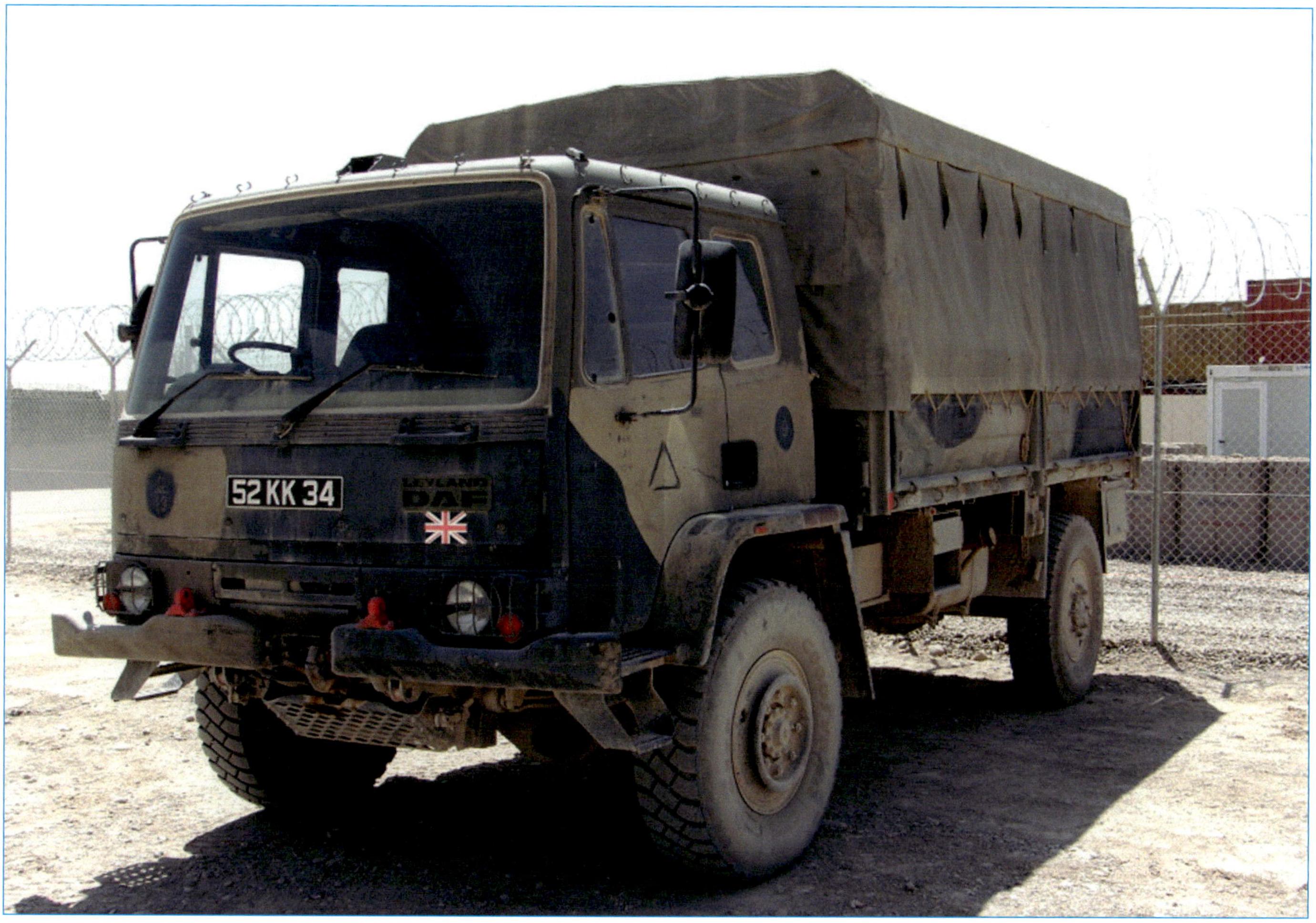
52 KK 34
LEYLAND
DAF

Engines, Electrical Equipment & Instruments

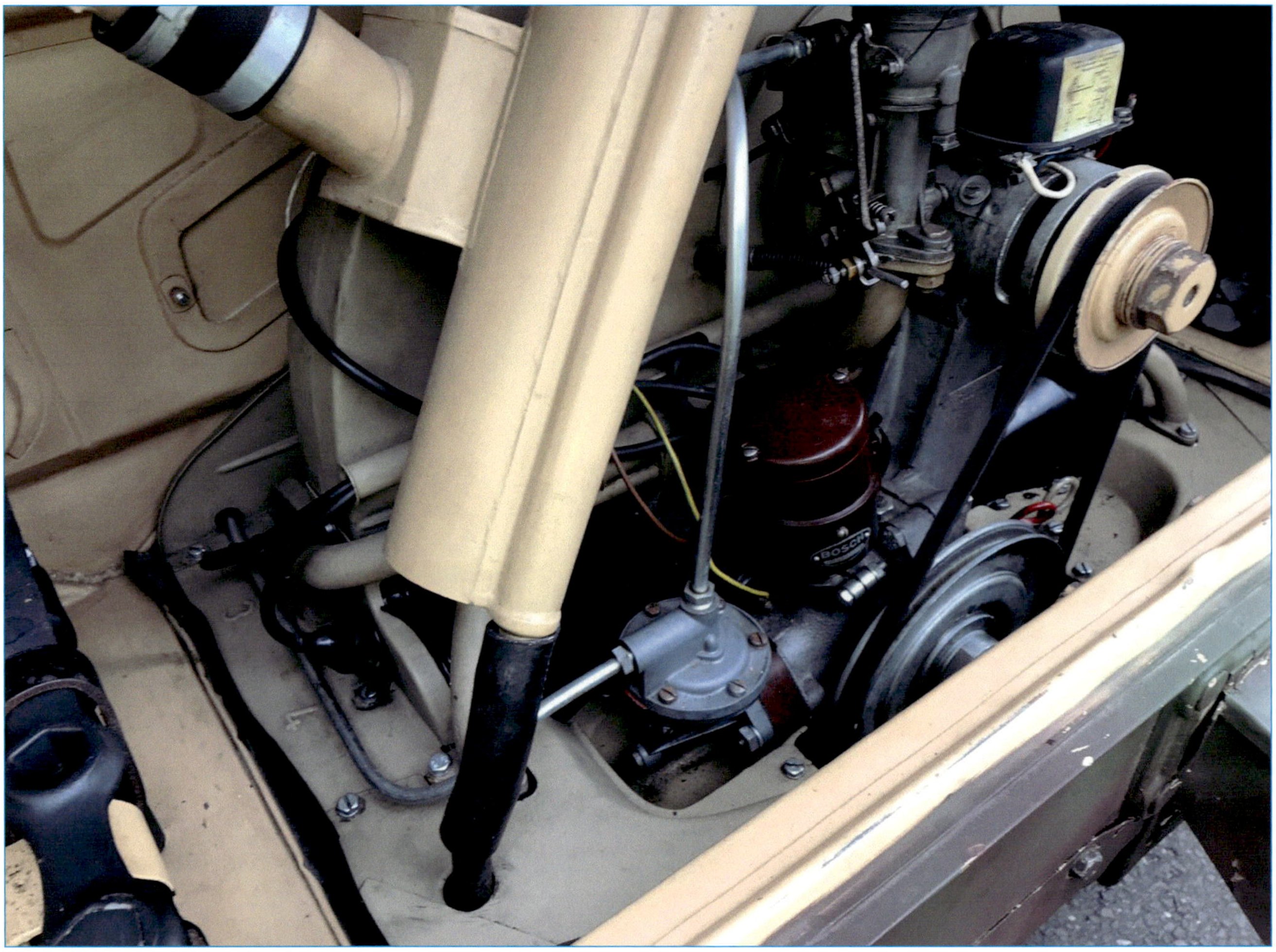

00 NC 37

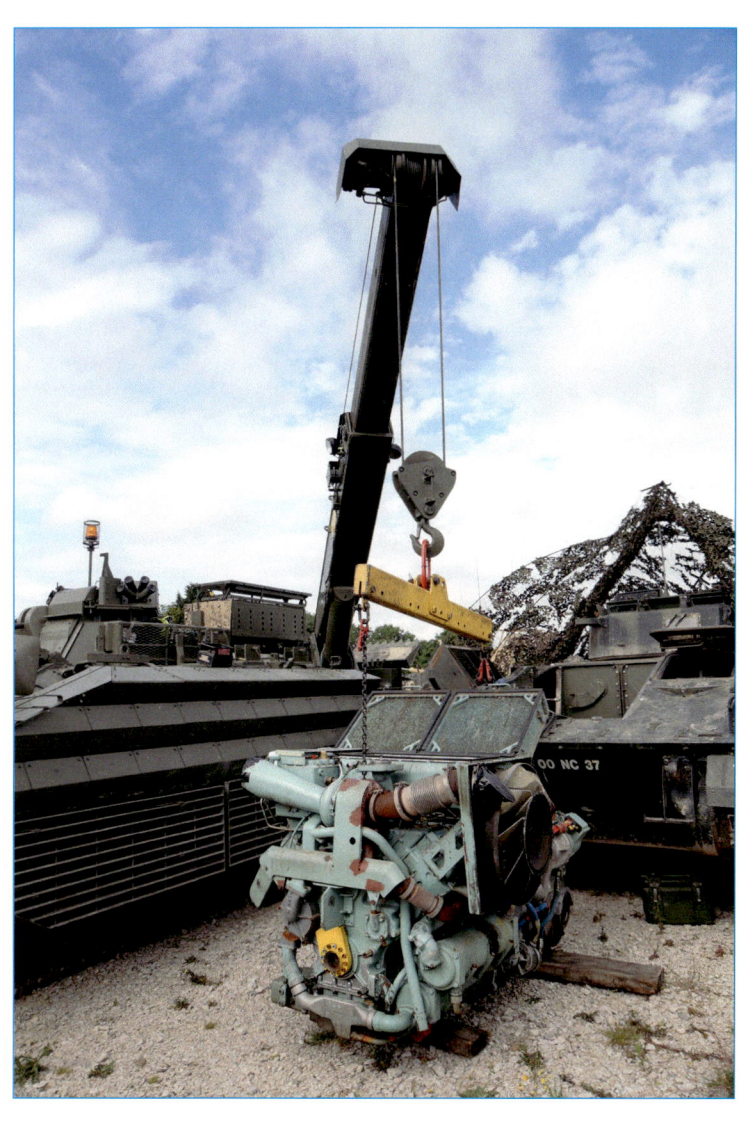

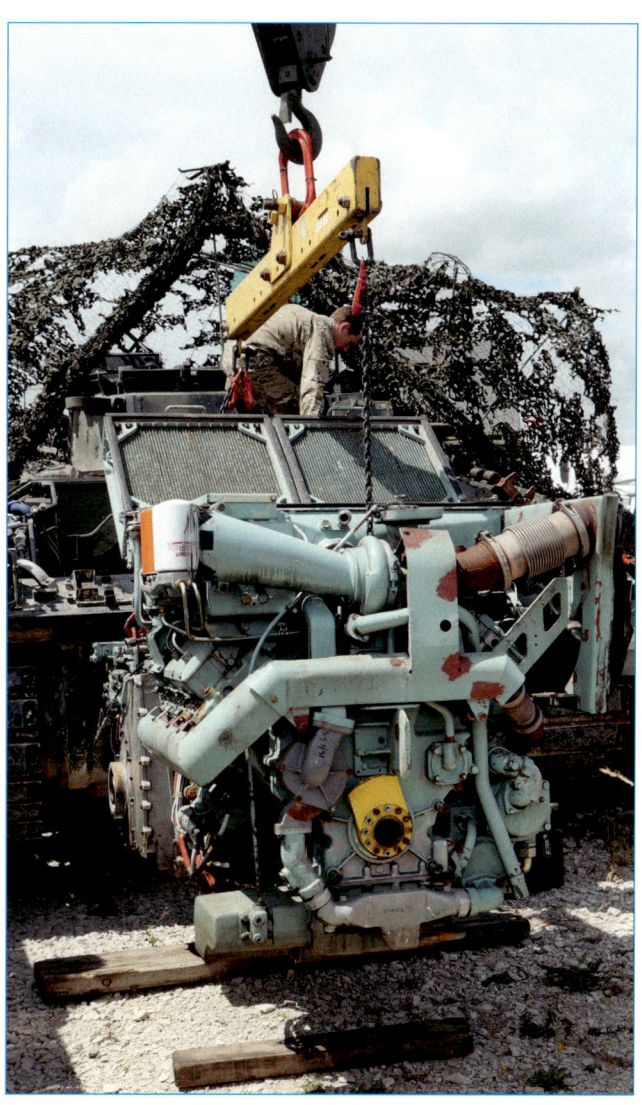

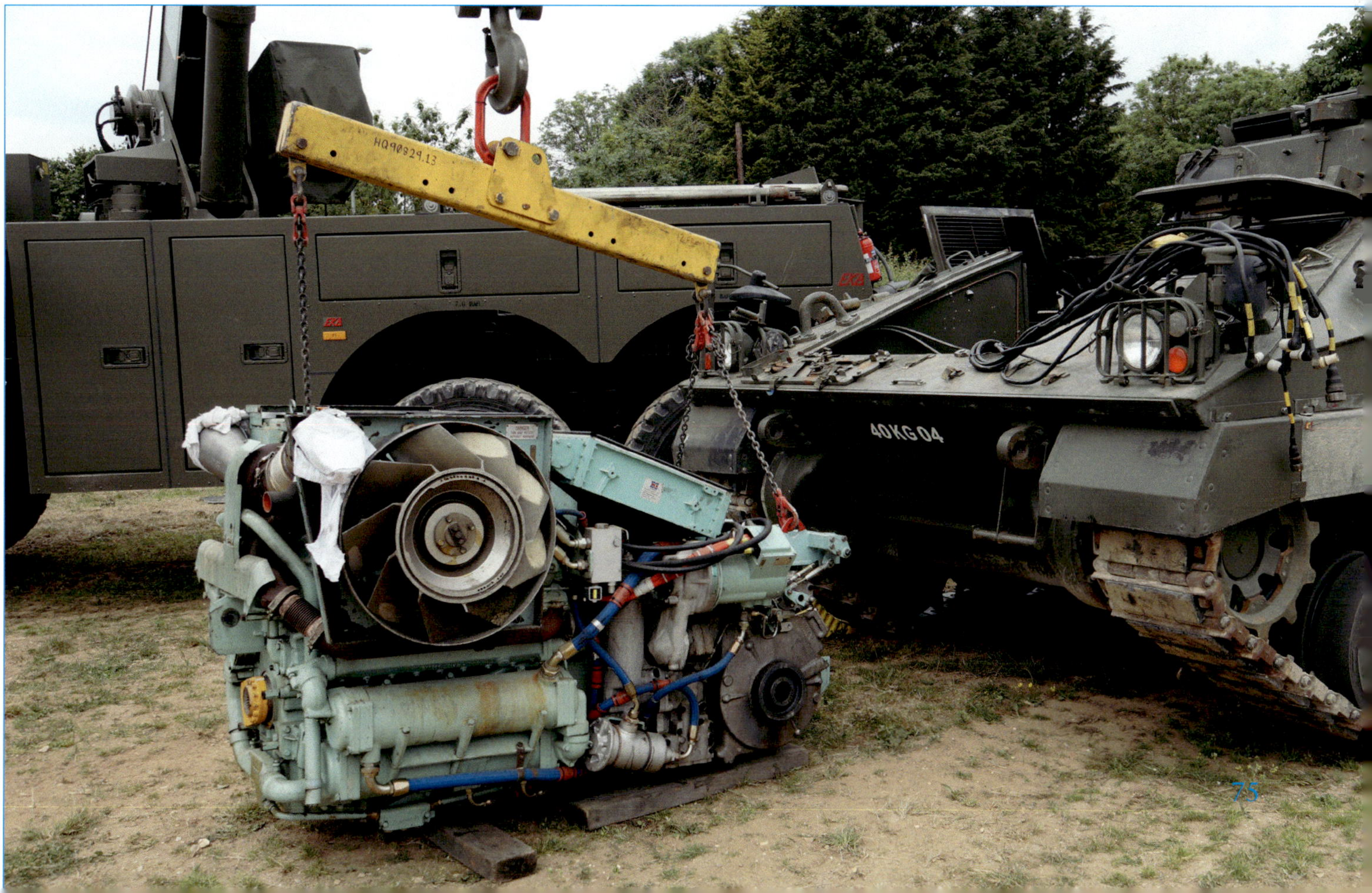
HQ90829.13
40KG04

77

86

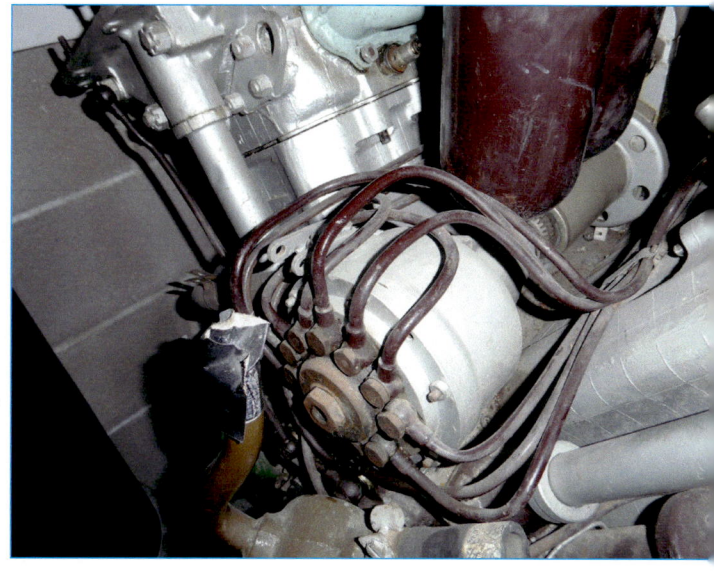

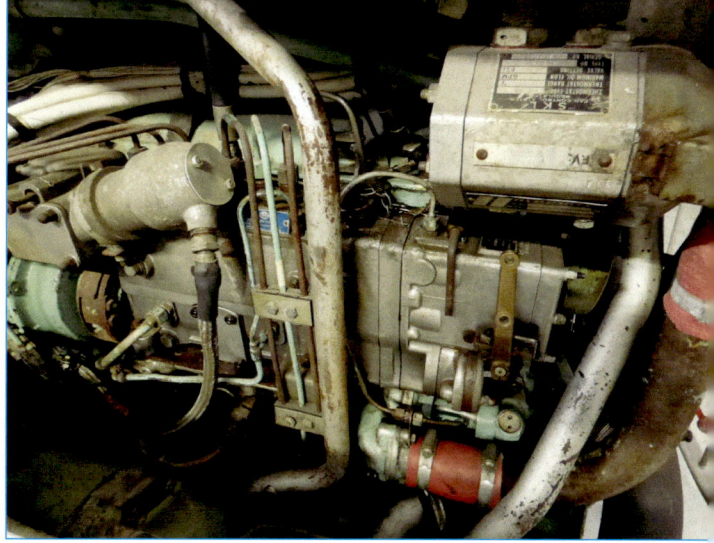

Engineer and Plant Vehicles

100

104

Glass and Sights

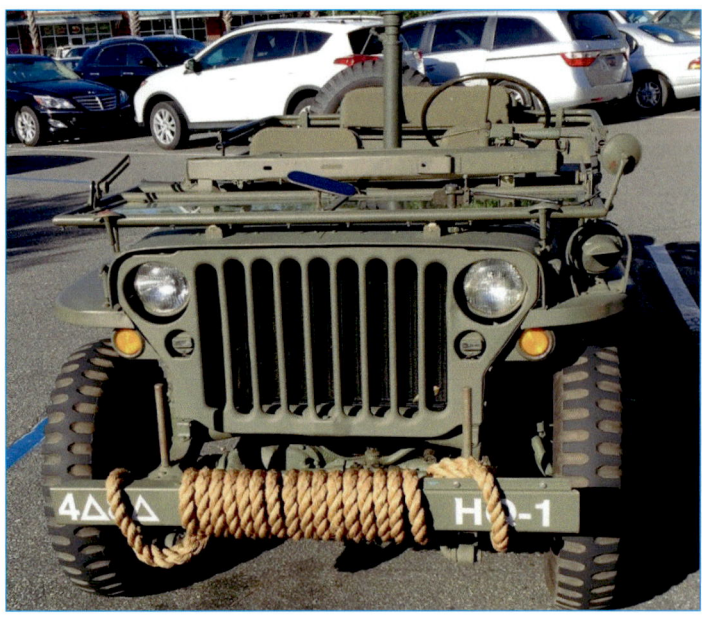

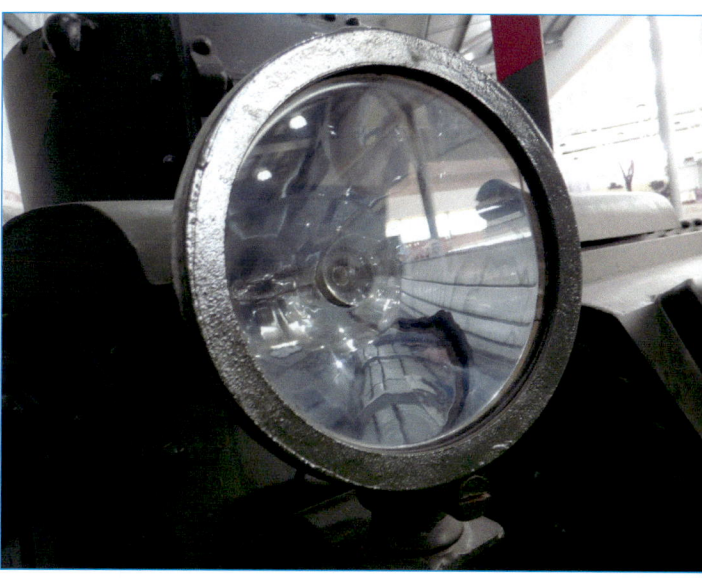

Extreme Rust

123

127

129

Miscellaneous

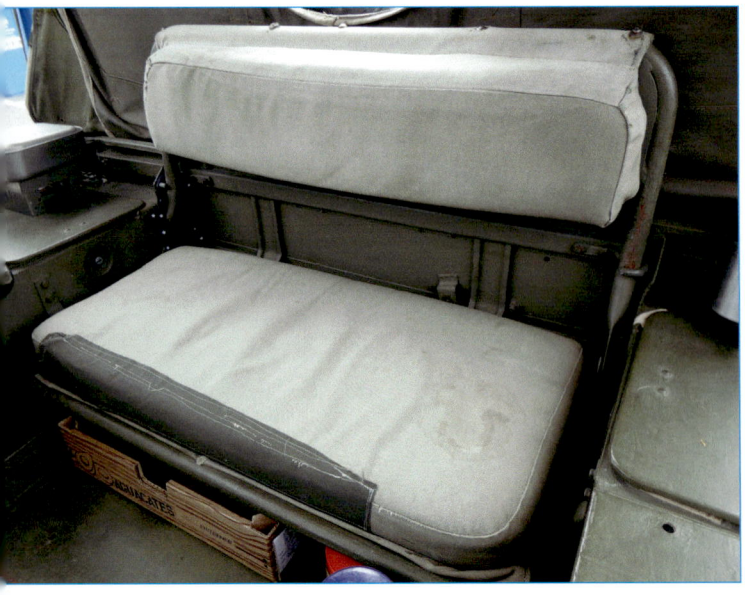

141

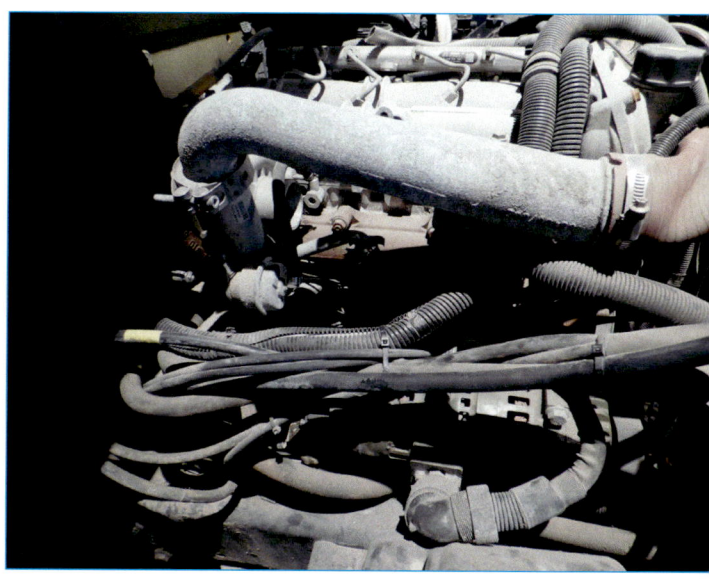

143

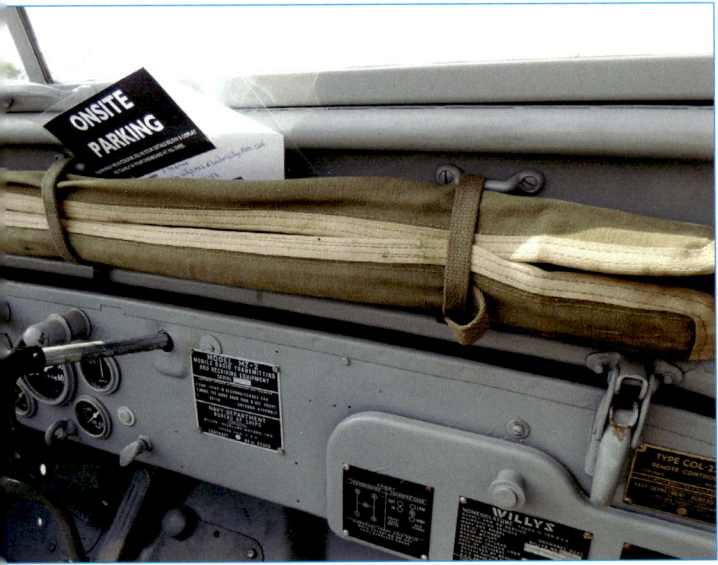
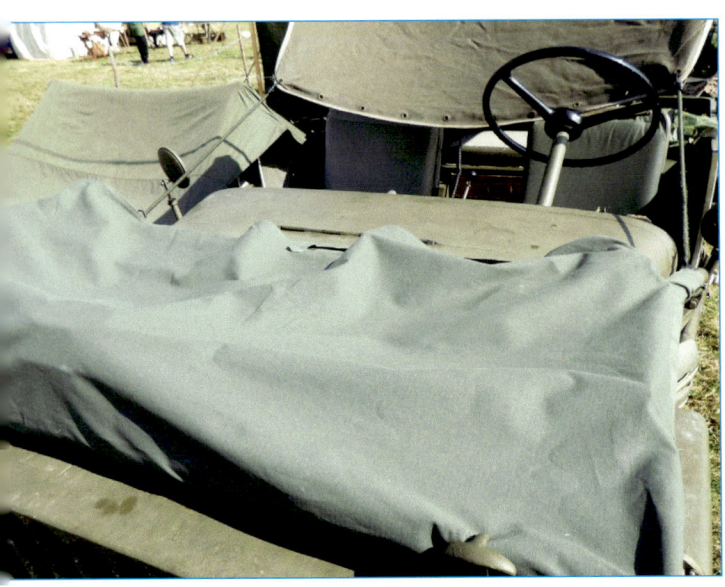

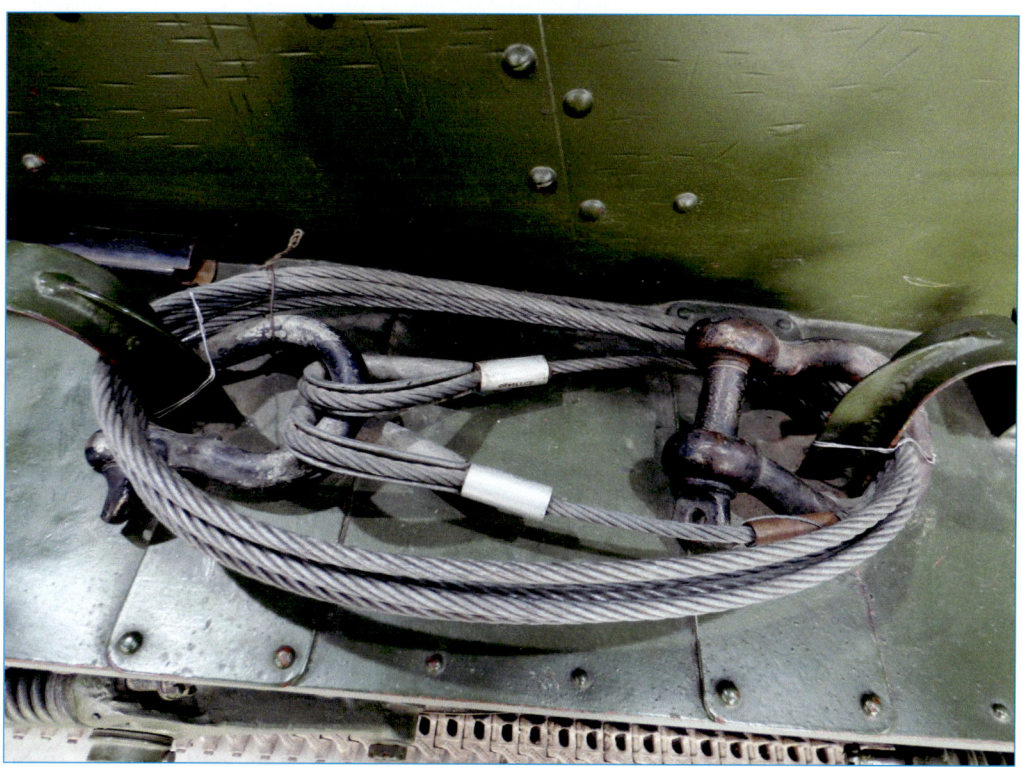

151